Affiliation

Mira Mattar

SAD PRESS

Bristol 2021

ISBN: 978-1-912802-39-5

For my family

كُن كالحُبِّ عاصفةً على شَجَر
- محمود درويش

Be like love - a storm among trees
- Mahmoud Darwish

Letter from Amman I
2015-2016

It is a spherical pleading from all sides – depthy, familial,
brown eyes widen, glass over when I say I have no
feelings about my uterus, its slick and bellicose
functioning. Detach. Repeat. Mostly there is a chalky
white row to swallow and get on the bus with, sinking
into its lovely geometric popper-infused upholstery, bones
rolling at my toes. This delicate, reliable bleakness, this
warm, bilious romance: cosiness. Grey, yeasty and damp. A
hand on the throat of one feeling passing only between
two people. No, bloated in one and gushing from the other.
Stone and sweat. Sweet and stoned. How the cunt gets
worshipped but they can't stomach (the word)
Mother. It is your doltish glee and not you that is
adorable. Your specificity is only that because you feel,
they must be alive. Pay me then! Vague and clumsy
sadist. Nice dumb wet robot. Chick pea, pumpkin, peanut
butter, cream; whip, eucalyptus, poison. Homely emotion
inside tracked daily for flinching, monitored annually for
blinking, for doubt or contempt. Leaving a temperate sea
for a hostile ocean, trading tawdry, sunlit glamour
for buttoned-up, stewed gloom. Sit for five years crying
and getting spit at. Call home to ask how to make spaghetti
without them knowing you're still only 22, without them
knowing you're forever perched on your suitcase because
they're laughing at your accent, because there are no
lemons. To be misunderstood and without lemons
is a terrible loneliness breeding in the bowels, forcing
the domestic loop's alluring stranglehold around your better
life, your tubed tomatoes. Your rent is paid – oh but there
were figs and pistachios, seasons and neighbours oh. This
is a remarkable location darling. Not bad for a camel-fucker
they laugh as the fist comes. More free market milk
than you'd ever seen. Here. There. Every home is a war
zone anyway. Where our each feathery unfelt pre-thoughts
are osmotically absorbed by one another, strung up

1

and paraded as intimacy, twisted into cruelty at mealtimes,
tugged through what has been sacrificed for opportunity.
What we swallow to survive. What we lose, weeping
hulks on the curbs of shot cities. We'd carry water up
11 flights of stairs. Never leave unless you have to.
What new motorway, what new beachfront condos,
what untreated sewage, what hovering four by fours,
what filled in bullet holes, what sudden street names now
necessary in the unnavigable sprawl? The minor must
populate, the walls hiccough Jesuses. Be miraculous.
It is inside your dwindling name. By freedom we didn't
mean owning the same frying pan for a decade or writing
profitless poems from left to right. Is it better
to be gracious and temper each word, to censor and iron
and know what was lost, to arrange your assets seductively,
your brain lucratively, or still to be visibly squirming, ugly
with the not-enough that turns all that farewell
into a narrow, tedious hoax?

Letter from Amman II
2016

You may be loving a murderer right now
starched and ironed by imported domestic workers
vetted, uniformed and eating later alone but of
the same one headphone in for the baby there
while on real hips a stranger's little man licks
the floor in his suit and tie. In organised cuteness
bows flop accented americanly and peaceful so far
about genitalia until the girl behind learns sexy.
The womb swallows cream directly from the source
clogs the mouth in time for tinted windows, dim-out
blinds, double-locked alarmed safety-belted
diazepam-laced genuflecting Mother Mary laminated
under the pillow shrouded densely with the distance
necessary to survive the distance which follows you
in the parking lot and then out of it and then to your
street and then to your door until you are safely within
your dwindling tribe violent with pride. Even the rectum
won't give insomnia a rest. Their work is tireless. God
bless them. Fatigued fatigues. Slim moustached. A
salute to their bravery. What bravery to preserve things
as they are. To adore to death. To spray and mop. To
check the rearview mirror, the wing mirrors, the
compact, to check the rearview mirror, the wing
mirrors, the compact, to check the rearview mirror,
the wing mirrors, the compact. Until each wrinkle
happens before the eyes, before the blood of Christ
stains the rug, before the overseas guests balk at the
burning garbage or a man starves to death legless
in a doorway. Just to be sure gargle with bleach after
every odour. Ensure no texture is textured. That no
light comes in in the morning. Ever pressing the iron
along the vast balloon of underwear or the narrow hem
of expense or the immense floral bedtime. Scratch out
the eyes until it is only holes and wondering why
there are holes when so much has been stuffed with

puppies and Jesus. Sickening at every corner of the
bathroom measured against piles of hand-stuffed
and rolled vine leaves arranged hugely, lined with chops,
steamed, flipped and returning in the white bowl ever
gleaming. Cif-scrubbed, nails protected. Hair up. On
the knees and groaning to rise from the endless wipe.
The darkening nipple drags behind a gorgeous exhale
is the closest to prayer's song on the knees facing Mecca
unrolled at 11.43am between the shoppers. A parrot
repeating translated repeating translated. Cup of milk.
Bread and its lack. What arrogance to refuse it. Kiss the
ground. Slim moustache. Keep the eye trained along
the barrel of things as they are, along the border
with our well-armed neighbour-in-peace who diverts
our river's water, drying our farms and shrinking
the shrinking Dead Sea. Long guns pirouette down
by the demographic I could add to were I born
of the big dumb brain of a man terrified into pride
and calling it independence, puffing its chest out as it
reaches emphysemically for dessert in 1946
the British. The old days. How grand the stairs were,
how the bougainvillea erupted like the first television,
how we crouched in the yard burning cotton buds
and wanting to be fucked, how they could double park
drunk and high with the spoilt confidence of wealth,
how we knew everyone and everyone knew us.

Letter from Amman III
2017-2018

Loving Englishmen was proving bad for my health
again. My hairs were greying and not elegantly. Sleepless
this season of gift-giving and almost blind in one eye. The
eldest's pain is unceasing, the odd and shooting one
of tendons. A nervous affliction cross-legged on the bed.
Sacs filling with liquid, misunderstood and approaching
the smooth hollows of pelvis, that genius construction.
Face treated for two hours with masques and creams,
gels and peels until the years are shed and below is that
baby self still squealing. Enduring want. I dreamt
my face was covered in bandages which when unravelled
revealed that nothing was wrong and I accepted my face
as my face and liked it. Everything ends. Those who
cannot share, leave – poisoning (the word) freedom.
To take it from is to not really have it. To think
it is a thing to be had is to deny it thoroughly. I have
seen the best women of multiple generations etcetera
etcetera. Bedtime sexless bedtime. It's like when you
talk there's this fly – and at vastly different latitudes
and longitudes the equivalent swatting and stuffing. I
would rather patent brutes than these excuses for friends.
You cannot return an embrace with your arms tied
behind your back, with your legs bound at the ankles,
you can only wriggle like a dumb hungry snake made
of holes bending backwards for the only option little slut,
spoilt spinster, pitied foreign cousin's anaemic lovers,
cold tomatoes, work clothes crushed round the
calves or half over the head and choking by midnight.
Move here and teach, move here and breed, move here
and eat all the figs you like. A nice man. You'll be
taken care of. (Which tells me assassination is certain.)
Unceasing, the work of women. Your lighter skin,
this spotlessness, this nourishing, this family Skype,
this hand in this sock, this goodnight kiss. In the
rearview mirror the tragedy of my barrenness. My

uncuddleable syntax. Beautiful but I do not
understand. My every creeping valentine. I am
loved best as a lusty sarcophagus. It would be sensible
to freeze your eggs though you are still only 17 to me.
I was twice that then and have yet to hear my insides. I
remember when sex was unmonitored before it moved to
the Continent. What future? What holds these streets
together is the thin film of tradition, which is the
thinner one of fear, which is the thinnest one of
power, which is the opaque one of kings, which is
the transparent one of mandates and colonies, which is
the invisible one of God which amounts to a
16 year old Palestinian girl slapping an IDF soldier
in the face because he shot her 15 year old cousin
in his head at close range with a rubber-coated
steel bullet, which lodged in his skull, broke his jaw
and put him in a coma in December 2017. An open
hole inside of which a bust pipe spurts is sealed
within two hours. They laugh and say ok, but the pipe
below's still burst. This is a nice neighbourhood.
This is where beggars keen between the cars, ask
low-toned for bread as we feast on baby birds and fruit
platters and continue suckling at the bones of kings.

Letter from Amman IV
2019

No wonder you're squirming. Earlobes and baby
toes lined along the threshold door flung open on
a solid wall of wasps circling back to the burglar
bedroom to pray hard to Mary, to Scheherazade,
to Philomela, to every woman who told stories
to survive. Is that what you'd always been doing little
soldier of worry? Scratching your song, wringing
sanity from your fermenting guts and nobody knows
why your tummy hurts. Cold gel of the ultrasound.
Spread of warm olive oil. Waiting belly up for Teta
clutching a stack of pirated videos where the beds are
pushed together, gap stopped by a rolled towel. Cool
strawberry sheets, whiskey and the adults round the
First Gulf War on TV. On a cousin's baby door
a homemade poster of Saddam, *Iraq* scrawled in
infant gracelessness emerging from a station wagon
in '93 the day The Oslo Accords were signed after
swimming club with Holly's mum going *your parents
must be very happy* something important happened
sloping past the English pansies, their name from
the French for thought, *pensée,* a symbol of
remembrance, mostly mine are someone else's –
                    I regularly put my hand inside
the fog Mama hates the damp here but adores
the trees, marries a man whose name translates to
Help Me Rain, tends her orchids remarkably
hardy Mama what will have burned down today?
What words must I spray paint over in the alleyway
down to school? Dirty Arab smash your face in,
stretch your hair into the playground, gel it small
and file your nose flat, ping pong bra strap tarmac
accent house smells funny house smells of lack.
Model student burns and slices, paper bags,
McDonald's straws, charred teaspoons, Rizlas,
Malibu – if they ask again say camels: three humps

is a Rolls Royce, two is a BMW, one's a Ford. It's
ignorance only - outswim them all, dream in two
tongues, it's ok you know how to breathe. We needn't
know each estuary, each dessert but we must know
what they did and do.

                  Fishes, grapes, encyclopaedias -
why then can I strum the tendons of your front
neck like a oud then? Why then if you ever sleep
do you not recall your dreams? and you - you really
didn't speak till you were five? Underwater I get
to be a needle. What is a man without memory?
Is it bliss he resides in, is it fantasy, is it the present?
What elastic terror is always pulling him back? By
which I mean: is he dangerous? By which I mean,
am I? and we're full of their half memories, our
bowels a portal sick and revolting, a tunnel dug
to another's story searing our organs - to Jaffa 1948,
to Amman 1955, to Kingston upon Thames
in the 1990s: wave machines and chicken nuggets,
shag bands and River Island, to the posh pool
of a long summer in West Amman: French fries
and jackknife dives - his whole body hair-pinning up
into the cyan sky and down the lethal edge of the
deep end: it was not only that I wanted to be svelte
and precise and a man, it was that I wanted to be
a blade: for my whole body to be a decision
instead of an option, a weapon, an uncrossable
edge. I wanted also to be only in water, eternal
and not yet born. In chlorinated arcs a feeling
of freedom pushes into my brain expanding me into
a puddle, a pond, an ocean, a predictable
desire for flight, no: a desire for an impossible
movement, an as yet unimagined one or: the
moment of its conception is the moment of its
realisation.

                  In my lonesome high up dawntimes
I conjure my ideal scent: ashtrays and cardamom,
Elnett and acetone, tar, jasmine, hash, lemons,

cum, chlorine – the smell of weapons that strip
and shred all life of any living seeps into my
daydreams even. I close my face against them
and wake to the ongoing dispossession and murder
of my kin and yes I'd contain the same if we were
strangers. We go from air-conditioned house
to air-conditioned car to air-conditioned house,
eat meat whenever we like, shop at Zara and H&M –
I don't even know what I'm missing half the time
I'm two hours ahead under a different sky at a
different kitchen table. The ordinary foreigner
ache striates the spine herniating discs for attention.
       The other end of the word
for heart is a call for a somewhere in which
to exist in mutual fullness, is a very practical
cry for destruction constructable only in the
lunch breaks of right now, from the top deck
of the 176, while we bury our friends, as your
glasses steam up over the big cook to last all
week; is a very necessary call to become audacious
as a chief ecstatic duty without which withers
and palls the easy fact that only from here does
an elsewhere come.

Affiliation
(for my father)

In the flameless, English suburb a young girl
                    opens windows
onto a brick wall. Sheet
        of sky enters. No sea, no
horizon, fragments
        of men own the neighbourhood.
                    If you crane your neck into a bird
            on the ledge of the tonsillitic balcony
            you slept on as a child
            you will almost see the sea (there
                    there) behind the American University.
The young girl climbs from one window
        scales carefully the exterior sill
            (honeysuckle, Silk Cut Silver,
            McDonald's milkshake halfway up the straw)
        and enters again through the other
            in an infinite loop
            or an ordinary circle
                    compulsively
            she exits and enters
            danger and names
            this motion being herself.
Rooftops puncture
                    the expanding lung
of this Better life –
        pesto, chicken Kievs, Channel 5
Paula Danziger, Stephen King, Judy Blume
        cotton bud, soap scum, shower cap
            we peek inside the neighbours' bathroom
        to check if we are human too
            to check if we are doing it right
            to check why no one
                touches anyone

10

except the people they have sex with
and therein is all their tenderness
spent again the turquoise dome, the emerald guts
of a shimmering life made probable.
Auntie, auntie can I be you?
Chain-smoking Kit Kats
in the bedside pyramid
of duty-free Kents
dangerously nice slipping
out of my mind
and down to the southern border
heavily armed
wires attached to my temples
at a facility in Eastbourne
where the baby brother's
convalescence was funded
where I said yes
come see the Arab
where I said yes
soldiers stopped emerging from toilet bowls
chasing me, chasing me
I drive faster
and faster, all the way to Russia brother
turns the fist
of a Chaunsa mango inside out
Fairuz shucks the oyster scooping
sawdust city boy
puts it to his mouth ignoring
mother while the bombs fall into his pockets
flowing with the American current, *Yes*
Prime Minister a Sunni
since the National Pact
your life since '48
kept being waiting for it to stop
so you can return –
home, to work, to your father, to normal, to the dog
left on that patch of earth

11

in a shaft of settled light cleansing
the fullness of ordinary life catastrophically and
without reservation, Bantustan camouflaged
invasion is a structure
not an event
by any other name expansive,
exterminating, eliminative, extractive
indicative of genocide is not an emotional claim
but a process, the settler
is not an immigrant beholden
to Indigenous laws, decolonisation
has no synonym
apartheid is not a proper noun
it evades and erases its own name
'apartheid' '~~apartheid~~' '[   ]'
but re/names with impunity streets
and sand dunes casually
but targeted as you cower
in the roofless kitchen
your arms up mute child
pins the racist boss against the wall deferentially
hotboxing tiny cars off the M25
listening to Nick, to Geoff
watching *Porridge* under the ungrateful cubicle
slurping fat eels
east of the City's
coke dripping body
carried over your shoulder and out of the desert
and down to the river
where I saw my well
irrigated fromness at last
ever thirsty farmers in the Jordan Valley
their water siphoned and redirected into
a single settlement peach
contains 140 litres of virtual water
appropriated from Palestinians
pitching from behind a burning car
in West Beirut a Molotov cocktail in an arc

12

on the trading room floor
        gestures towards
        wealthy classmates' used-once textbooks for sale
                cream skimmed for the street cats
                you send me pictures of
      'thought of Olive'
          Zaytooneh, of course the foreigners
        have made a charity for the cats here
           while the legless
             beg on the curbed
        stub of national debt
          vacationing at a permanent distance
      from tear gas Made in France by SAE Alestex
        hurled also at the gilets jaunes
        cannisters, CM6 grenades,
    G1 'random motion' grenades
      impossible to pick up and throw back
        loosen up you think everything is racist!
      Annihilation, exploitation,
       the sand under my desk,
    the words you hear
  when they think they are alone
or you are one of them palely
  photocopying hot pink worksheets
    in a West London basement
dumbstruck at the words
    at the impressed guffaws
at the infected gall of saying it
  come on we were all thinking it
    doubly my jaw at the word
whose wasp drew
  twice, no, squared
      up to the fury
        which protects the love
      silent at is core free
      to yell 'Lawrence!' at sunburned Englishmen
        with t-shirts on their heads in the summer
        free to sell our labour

free to be part of this glorious System
to know the worth of our selves
(do we ever mean the same thing with
the most important words?)
but never to a lover –
on our knees in bathrooms internationally
dependent on a disguise of sovereignty
of nation French accented father
I've never had a decent pomelo in the UK
what do they do with all that water?
We play nice for the American tap   USAID! USAID!
store it in rooftop tanks
for IDF soldiers to piss in next door
collude in the Dead Sea's contraction
mine for potash and magnesium
7000 sinkholes and counting,
surface almost halved since '76,
300km squared of seabed exposed
the myth blooms beneath
the West Bank Mountain
Aquifier diverts 80% of Ramallah's rain
his citrus orchards
his swimming pools
an orange ball thunking
in a summer palm
in a city wetter than London
listener heed your fantasy
today there is more blood than water in Gaza
scarcity is not evenly distributed
when Mekoret charges a West Bank Palestinian
more than a settler
on their knees and warring neighbours in 18 sects
plus immigrants, domestic workers and labourers
haram, pity keeps the object object
12 men in one room as long
as there is never a cloud in my glass
returning to their quiet yellow cheese
and glinting rose gardens

their military avenues slick
with marron glacé they left us this combustible Paris
restructured child
you are floating through dusky pink
taupe-ish pre-dark-web-MDMA, thin-armed
and improvising nutrition
at High Easter, St Faith's Road, SE24
where the kitchen sky was ten thousand swifts
to smooth the hair of
after they puke into an Iceland bag
on the top bunk
sleeping in a pile
at 175 Coldharbour Lane
rolling backwards in through the first floor window, child
when will you come back?
The chicken is gathering dust
your tonsils are ringing
in love and dedicated
primarily to deciphering how the lilacy
pastel of hydrangeas can also be electric
Mama
can't you see I am busy
deciphering how the lilacy
pastel of hydrangeas can also be electric?
Mama
I am learning to see
have you ever seen
a bluebell wood Mother these English
taught me flannels and butter,
language and forests Mother
when was the last time
you came here in Spring?
You think it is always one colour, a desert
sad, dry   you deny it   (me) (you)
seeing only the impression of a season
then running, child
you have to be inside the System
enjoy your flexible passport

I cannot tell you how many passports I have striven for
but you were born a citizen   (not alien, not refugee)
of this still world
before the law
changed fully documented ingrate
as if it were a universal category: citizen
occupied resident, refugee, foreigner,
immigrant, just never a national
when nation is race concealed
colonial difference built
up stand out blend in slide
into the schema of a luxury
and stop taking everything so seriously!
Perhaps you were right because here
I am here   a Palestinian first or nothing
at 36 waiting here   but only until
every morning to be born here   and only because
again with the birds here   it is an expansion
what more could I want
cradling, binding, carrying at least
a freedom of feeling
a parakeet, a crow, a pigeon
a withness
not of trade, of speech
but for our living
not to be only a problem to be solved
look –
I was never privately ashamed of really wanting
us to really want
to be alive
(especially that time in Queen's Park of all places)
how it came as an outside feeling
and how I housed it
and it grew
and I became a house
with all its windows open
and ivy coming in
and brambles

and it grew
but I could not tell it:
that I wanted to be alive.
So much so that I understood
the desire for immortality
(looking into your otter eyes)
that I understood
(on a mattress on Norwood Road,
the ceiling bulging with water)
that the favourite psychic chokehold of this place
is humiliating
that feeling into silence,
cynicism, bumbling, acceptance,
apology, passivity, control,
into smashing the glass against the wall
and the chair against the door
and the head against the shaking
clutch of nerves those noises –
dull, damp, afraid
big boys
making a mess of language
mistaking erudition for truth
scholarship without commitment is just commerce
commitment without love is just posturing
to assume you are adding to the world by filling it
by pinning it
down by force
you are taking more away
to fix things as they are
is not to heal
your frightened heart
little man
how can you speak at all?
(At least I know I am terrified
of saying anything out loud.)
When I learned one of my favourite flowers
was just the name of the man
who pointed at it hardest

and in that pointing, claiming
and in that claiming, naming,
I imagined every flower and plant
and creature and tree was only
an anagram of blue-eyed Adam, of God,
father the gardens withered,
I made a vow of silence very loudly
and threw language to the ocean
then spent my life swimming.
So how could I speak without knowing
the history of each word's world
and each world's words?
I would have to understand motion.
This gorging, this hoarding
how can we divest from this economy
that thwarts us banking
on our terror of the gorgeous void
which only liars fear
that makes touch possible
for without air there is no fire
to stay beside eviscerating
emptiness that knows the way
that is the way,
the guide, the fire I stay beside
and name that staying I
and name that I wit(h)ness
and name that wit(h)ness
those three little worlds
Every Girl Is Dying
To Hear:
I don't know
in the first-person plural
I don't know but I want to make it
with you.
That outside feeling grew but I could not tell it –
especially your friends bear down on language
I do it too, we go around
ripping each other's tongues out from the roots

the radial beam
spit blood up into the gutter
outside Sainsbury's Waterloo, turning our pockets out
for ourselves, for our friends
sleeping to death in the street –
oh freedom! Oh System!
Oh eco washing up liquid!
Clean us back into the garden
with the lowly hand strip
us of what keeps pressed down
the most crucial feeling is
imagining
dismissed as fantasia
as madness medicated
which as it rises is caught
and redirected into a slimline care of only
the perimeter of self
as if our veins ended in us
the local boundary bolstered
by its attendants: the partner
and the tenderising lover,
the community, the tribe calculating
degree of deviance and how to quell it
how to make it fecund and compatible,
the home wherein it perishes bed sore and flatulent
with comfort
with need flung
and faded, pressed against
the photocopier fumbling thrilled
lays down at the surface of skin only
as if our veins ended in us
an abyss
What, you think you are too good for our sorrow variations?
Containing so much at the top of the stairs
this adolescent foreigner meeting your eye
oh you, you and your sea!
What because you live in 'the West'?
That blindspot slaughtering

your life is better than an English dog's
never having to see itself at least
summers are hot in your country!
(What country? What country?)
oh fire eviscerate, water cull –
Emilia, I saw that man on Blythe Hill Fields
trying to fly again
and enjoyed my cavities and mealtimes best alone
look, don't worry –
I have my little fears percolating
behind my every blinking eye
but I am not hallucinating
just because I hear everything
twice or more I thought
it's what you wanted too? This
being here, it vacillates for both of us I think
the managers are global after all
I am well practiced in wanting what hates me
Baba I don't want saving
not even after work
not even beneath the lavender sky exposing
the lie of geography
at the peripheries' core –
three words can say it:
drinkable tap water
but when I send you an article about
Flint, Michigan, USA
you do not know where to file it
because then there really is no place
left on earth at all
and you will have to concede
and concede to me:
the baby of the family
and a girl.

Who hears (your) voices in the dark and listens till morning
with an easy heart resisting

those galloping energies that catch and turn
what liberates into what dominates
the streets of your city
burned again and again
into the retina of my education
my professor's eyes keep darting
to our chests front row double crossed
and at night we unpeel our schooling meticulously
to the edge where we could think from
knowing that what would not meet without a lie to join it
was exactly where learning began
with irreconcilability
with a nail in the bed
and then we slept like a baby
and woke up
held
and thrilled by every
gasp of light
knowing at once
that not matching the category revealed
not that I was a lie
somehow breathing flesh
but that the category was –
a weapon
and that our being proved it
knowing at once
our knowing is history
a map tied
in soft rupture to the inner eye
compulsively entering and exiting
as water moving against
the biggest tenders were fourfold
1. fuel income and distribution 2. food importation
3. biometrics and digital technology 4. management of waste
flowing directly into the sea every second
mercury, cadmium, copper, lead
frothed blood lapping again the coast
of An Ancient City For The Future

whose shit you can literally see from space
dear brother, comrade, a star
a phoenix
as though recovery were life
arcing through a black sky
weeping in short elastic bursts
there is no triumph here we slurp
the ends of our pomegranate-orange juice
and chuck the plastic cups and straws into some hole
I cannot know if my hand on your shoulder
is doing anything at all
we cannot know the depths
of rotten infrastructure
can only smell its shit
and when it rains hard in refugee camps people drown
or are electrocuted
by liquid lightning
tears in '91, 2015, 2019, 2020
how well she played the piano once
I had insisted upon coming I would insist again
because here you are almost all of you at once
and I can watch your hulking shadow
rippling, breaking
without the fine cut of geography between us
oh great interrupter
phantom lectern, table wine, veal
butchered, beaten, breaded, lemoned
choleric water, anemones' scrambling
velvet tendrils, stray kitten
scrounging fish guts, paying twice for water if you're
lucky
young girl
warm house
cream cheese silently
spread to the edges
layered with neat discs of cucumber
lightly satisfied at the baby blue Formica counter
with how they stick at 7.51am

22

before the mostly punctual bus
full of squirrels, full of screaming
foxes, look a woodpecker
folding a blueberry Pop-Tart
raw between two squares of toilet paper
for swimming club dreaming
of America, fantasising
automatically of getting to lose to the biggest winner
of getting to exist beside him in 2020
your pain is still bigger than mine –
I sucked it up,
black oil through a plastic straw.

I was extremely inconvenient on the hundredth day of the, yes, revolution
bringing an ancient horror to the family gathering
where the word 'thawra' was being trialled
in opulent surroundings –
how a word can be feared
how that fear can be a desire
how a desire can be feared
not wanting to say it
yet
or wanting to say it
to make it truer in naming
or does naming only pin down   (say Palestine, you must)
forty mages scratching the head of the tribe
three little dogs howling
eat yourself free
what a waste of a void
but no one stopped climbing into the streets
had I always been climbing from windows
waiting for friends to run with?
When a friend is nothing like you
but looking in the same directions
when a friend is not a category but someone to ask
what do we want with?
When a friend is often against you

honing what 'together' means and why
and where it begins
and that it ends
and in that ending grows
form
is not all muscle
but all of it is breathing
love big enough for everyone
to be separately angry about whatever they want
for as long as they need
which is the happiness that could be possible
if you are willing to have your own memories
if you are wise enough
not to conflate anger with aggression
there is your anxiety hounding you to the door
asking again and again
why can't I lift the weight of my limbs?
Do you really love me?
How do we make another world?
I am just standing in the kitchen!
I am just learning on my knees
in bathrooms internationally
that my submissiveness relied on the amnesia
upon which my popularity was built
fuck
I willed it
you, you are the one who cannot remember
his dreams or the soldiers
the auntie you ran to escaping the camps
the aeroplane, your father, the last boat, the old house
when the beginning of waiting to return in a month
began you sweet baby
of the family
mistaken for jolly
oh big bubble head balancing on some spine
I do not know how to have this condition
while riding the bus
trying to dismantle my nervous cathedral of self

while my lover severs my nipples
to use as chips to gamble with
                    I always loved an addict
      so my own worries would pall
AQA, EdExcel, OCR, IBS, HMRC,
        the Oxford comma, the 11-Plus, my budget,
      my mother, yours, that fucking broken pipe
I retreat
            into my secret longing
                  to be a carful of boys
            high and speeding
      in that royal blue Renault Clio
      fast as possible away
from the irresponsible project of home
                        it's a world I want or out of it
                  I mean the distance from loneliness
                        that renders it meaningless –
            a shell in your palm
                  important to have known
                  (to know how to be alone in the world)
      but impossible to remember
            its desolate winter beach
            or how it could ever be possible again
            for I have never been I
            and you have never been you
            and yet we are never we only
            or ever could be always
            a wild range of motion
                              in motion
driving down the finely tarmacked streets of
      Wimbledon, Streatham, Earlsfield,
Tooting, Wandsworth roundabout
      is an iconic superstructure smooth and silent
      tulip heads
      those little ginger biscuits from IKEA
ring pull cans of sweetcorn
      poking soaking rice
      in a yellowing Tupperware, nicotine

sweating in bronze streaks
ach finding a boy
to put his fingers inside you – for freedom
instead of your own
finding a boy
to push you too young against a wall and liking it – for freedom
instead of your own
silver lit edges
of geranium leaves
your own lovely face
suddenly illuminated behind the lighter flame
at an underage party in Twickenham seriously
what do we want for us?
You and me Teta, ketchup on our eggs
your hair growing back like a baby's
the last time I saw you in the hallway
falling half asleep
glasses on on purpose
because you love when she takes them off for you
and strokes the sublime planes of your face
occasional
DILFS of south west London
salmon shorts, popped Jack Wills collars
on Clapham Common
congealing unhappily into the fantasy of a standard shag
their wives
their children I teach at big oak tables
lovely massive sofas
£60 cushions
clean windows
the coaster sticking to my cup
as I sip humiliating me
adopt me, own me, mother
I am your age now but you keep getting younger
I up my rate to prove it
tell me is home a certain place?
Doubt has a bad reputation
tell me where the beginning of discernment is without it,

the beginning of thought
the beginning of walking home with bare arms
in a summer made wholly of jasmines
tell me how to move from the desire which owns me
garottes me in my sleep
to the desire which moves you in a total direction
without the war inside
bamboo this way, that, water,
dog, I like the cool grass on my bare back,
I love a few people very much
how do you end a circle?
Why do you fear a word?
It stokes the gap between your life and you
you are the baby too
and I wasn't making anything easier
tired, my bowels full of cotton
but I finally had energy to climb over the fence
to contain my cockiness about sea swimming
because secretly I decided not to die anymore
(in Queen's Park of all places)
or to get off on slightly dying all the time
because secretly I decided not to
take the blame anymore
for somebody else's nightmares
or for their dreamless nights
or for the neo-liberalisation
of the post-war Lebanese economy
being nine
realising one Barbie's cupped palm
fit perfectly over another's pointy breast
and that was my selfishness
and there was my freedom
and t/here was the gilded passport, and the
NHS, and the pavement that
does not just become a hole with a jagged metal pipe
sticking out of it ready to cut you up
whenever
and t/here was the orthopaedic pillow, and the

27

good immigrant, and the mirage
of fiscal accountability, free travel
for pensioners and responsible redevelopment,
    immense green spaces and hundreds of
homeless people in Lewisham, and another case of
    mass abuse in a children's home, in the church,
in a care home, in the bowels of Parliament,
                and t/here was no street crime but your wife
            is yours to rape and the priest is yours
        to bribe, and the Virgin is under my pillow, and
            the mosque is outside my window,
    and the beautiful shrine is between my eyebrows,
            and t/here was not civilisation
        when salvation is the subject of all history,
    I'm here for the churches officer I swear,
                and t/here was another pretty girl
            sobbing in a Pret, and
26 honour killings last year in Jordan and 80 women
        murdered by their male partners in the UK
        between 2018-19 and 2 billion people on earth
        living without basic sanitation facilities
and that is what happens when saying no becomes
        a luxury revealing the lethal force
        behind most options
                    watching you weep
                you watching me weep
    but never with a hand on my heart for My Country
                I have none, I want none
        what I want is never called nation
            that bourgeois phenomenon
        that end of imagination
            a suckling son
        even in that extreme case
    where my baby heart whispers
                I want I want I want
        even in that extreme case
        that shredded your father and mother
                your sister and brothers

28

your foetal expression
the neighbouring nations
even in that extreme case
that ran into your children
sick with unknown unknown unknown
other other other
that cuts us up
and cuts between us
like a jagged metal pipe sticking out of wherever –
affiliation.

Waiting for my favourite mother to diagnose me as no longer depressed
clutching my wonky spring onions
in the waiting room of Brockwell Park Surgery, SE24
studying the friendly painting
wanting to be part of the friendly painting
which was of the friendly world
and the friendly people in it
and the friendly animals
and the friendly trees
and the friendly traffic
and the friendly post boxes
and the definitely friendly sky
fuck it I thought
take me to that blue of blues –
diving I surface
a decade later
in another blue that kept unfolding
opening and opening and opening
the posters blown off the wall
by an Israeli rocket in '76
the rest of the semester cancelled
graduating in an empty room
smiling every day if even just to the face
distorted in the bathroom tap
plankton I am with you
I am with the fungus in my ears

stretching nasturtium I am with you
        getting told you're a whatever like me
told and told and told
    oh Katie, oh Annabel, oh Sally Anne –
things are terrible in the 'Middle East' aren't they?
Things are terrible in Putney, bitch
        things are terrible in the underpass,
    things are terrible in your neglected crevices
                                give not your life to things
                                throw things to the flood
                                all one in the end –
                                water
come quick I have swallowed my pills again
        come quick I swear I'm going to jump
                            ocean, take me, take me –
                            no, take this world.
            When I see you in Beirut I see you
            but to you can I only resemble?
                                Is that love?
                To eat oranges like your mother,
            some auntie's gestures,
                my hair a niece's.
                            Who do you look like?
                Who do you look like?
She, she saw me straight away
    and undid me in that seeing –
love balks at boundaries
    love grins at you smoking menthols in the early 2000s
            at an indie disco in Coventry
                                fuck.
                    I miss her.
            I miss her and I know it's practice for missing you.
I miss her and other things happen
                    things? Throw things to the flood
    or you look away for a minute
and a tree in Peckham Rye Park has ignored the metal
        railings and grown regardless
    distorting   them angelically
        resisting.

When I see me in the mirror I see you.
I study you in your occasional grace
scoring and peeling an orange,
halving and handing me segments
the top and bottom discs stacked to the side
oranges have everything I want
they are what they are all at once
their word, their colour, their fruit,
in English, in Arabic
what else can say that for itself?
What else constantly ceases being what it is not?
And yes I know I am a Jaffawieh
talking about oranges
and yes I know you think us
nostalgic
but for you there is only one type of memory
because there is only one type of time, a line
from barbarism to Europe
named knowledge
which for you is only singular
me here, you there
singular nouns
what knows can never be known
what is known can never know,
or better it can forget
you whose capacity for belief is only in things
because the thing cannot imagine
the thing cannot imagine freedom
this is your need fixed
you then complain of a lack of sensation
meanwhile the thing breathes
you call it an animal and want it
it leaves nothing out
it learns without forgetting
the phantom limb.

Late 2019
      in a few months I am meant to be going
There for the first time. I am to return
      a different person. I am to be alone
for a few days. I am to try
      to find the place you were born
which you cannot direct me to
         which you cannot return to
      which I am not welcome in
      which I do not know how to find
         a British citizen might have wept softly
      or felt an absence of feeling
         or an obscure one
      or a new one
or would perhaps have only needed to pee,
      eat, been too hot or too cold as usual.
What would have the hundreds of
      WhatsApp videos, thousands of email
forwards, triple walls of books,
      decades of conversation and
      years of education inside me meant
         standing 'there' alone?
You are of England now but never with it
      Oh England.
      Little idyll of your heart.
Whenever I return I feel the throttle
of organised pansies, the arresting silence,
their impermeability, their assuredness,
      immortals.
      But the more we imagine freedom
      or imagine being free enough to imagine it
      the more we realise we are wrong again:
      it is not that happiness and freedom
      are in relation –
      the one the child of the other
      as though we had only one mother
      it was that love and freedom were
      conditions of each other opening
         like a day

                              like morning
                              like water
when I have glimpsed those
    or tried to know them or known them
    glimpsing they have been a present continuous
            unfolding multiplying infinitely
like fighting, like dancing, like writing
            where motion, desire, thought,
            will, spontaneity
        are one and all at once in time.
            You said I do not belong
    to you or anyone, that like you
        I am of this world.
                Then my first act will be leaving
    so I can return, I said
            holding you gently by the radiator,
    so I can be with not I
nothing belonging to me either.
            And when this glimmers
                    sheer, a thread in the air
        half-invisible between us
    and between us and the world
                I know that that is like love
                stripped of violence and pride,
        shame, passivity, irritation, demand
        for sameness, happiness, unhappiness,
                so I call
        and maybe you listen when I speak
        and maybe I listen when you speak
                we might laugh
            discuss new salad dressings
            we've concocted
                    just a touch of soy sauce –
            little idyll of your heart
        give us your pavements, your queues,
    your councils, your floral arrangements,
    recycling, parakeets, forms, lane discipline,
        these railings, these gurneys,
                            these trees.

Notes

The epigraph to the collection, by Mahmoud Darwish, is from *Mural* (2017), translated Rema Hammami and John Berger. Cover image with permission from George Steinmetz. Sinkholes pock-mark the emerging shoreline of the Dead Sea near Ein Gedi.

Letter from Amman III
2017-2018

The incident I am referring to at the end of this poem is the story of Palestinian activist Ahed Tamimi and her cousin Mohammed Tamimi, who was shot in the head at close range with a rubber-coated steel bullet by Israeli soldiers who had forcibly entered the Tamimi home on 15 December 2017 attempting to quell stone-throwing demonstrators who were protesting the expansion of Israeli settlements in Nabi Salih. In response, Ahed, with her mother Nariman and cousin Nour, approached the two soldiers outside the Tamimi home and slapped, kicked and shoved them. The soldiers did not retaliate. The incident was filmed, went viral and drew global attention. Mohammed was put in a medically induced coma to treat his head injury and regained consciousness a few days later. On 19 December 2017 Ahed Tamimi was arrested in a night-time raid and 13 days later charged with assault, incitement and stone throwing, despite being a minor. On 24 March 2018, Tamimi agreed to a plea bargain with prosecutors whereby she would serve eight months in prison and pay a 5,000-shekel ($1,437) fine. While imprisoned she earned her high school degree.

According to Defence for Children International-Palestine approximately 500-700 children (12-17 years) are detained and prosecuted in the Israeli military court system every year. Children are often taken from their beds by Israeli soldiers in the middle of the night, and most are subject to physical violence during arrest, transfer or interrogation. The most common charge is stone throwing.

This information is predominantly from Ahed Tamimi's Wikipedia page and DCI-Palestine's Military Detention page.

Letter from Amman IV
2019

Although I started this poem in August 2019 with no dedication in mind, I dedicated it in October 2019, for publication in Lotte L.S.'s *No Relevance #1*, to the people rising up, revolting and resisting in Lebanon. It is now autumn 2020 and I dedicate it once again to the people of Lebanon, particularly those in Beirut.

When I wrote the phrase 'a feeling of freedom' I was thinking of Lisa Robertson's conversation with Laura Broadbent ('The Body is My Mysterious Concept' in *Scapegoat Journal*) where Robertson says (when speaking of hiding to read in peace in the ruined corn-silo on her parents' farm as a child): 'I wouldn't say that I found this place, or others, in a search of learning. It was more like a search for an emotion of freedom. This freedom-sensation has been aligned with certain architectures and economies. Reading and writing have at times become guides to this alignment, and so have friendship, cooking, travel, retreat, conversation, gardening – most of the Epicurean practices.'

Affiliation
(for my father)

1. 'invasion is a structure not an event ...'
'settler colonizers come to stay: invasion is a structure not an event.' Patrick Wolfe, 'Settler Colonialism and the Elimination of the Native', *Journal of Genocide Research*, 2006.

2. 'the settler is not an immigrant ...'
'Settlers are not immigrants. Immigrants are beholden to the Indigenous laws and epistemologies of the lands they migrate to. Settlers become the law, supplanting Indigenous laws and epistemologies. Therefore, settler nations are not immigrant nations.' 'Decolonization doesn't have a synonym.'
Eve Tuck and K. Wayne Yang, 'Decolonization Is Not A Metaphor', *Decolonization: Indigeneity, Education & Society*, 2012

3. 'apartheid is not a proper noun / it evades and erases its own name / 'apartheid' ~~'apartheid'~~ '[   ]''
'Unlike apartheid in South Africa, where all these kinds of proscriptions

36

were bluntly spelled out, what we see in Israel is racism that avoids or distorts language. That doesn't make it any less racist, however. Derrida was right to say that what distinguished South African apartheid was its brandishing of the word; what helps distinguish Israeli apartheid, by contrast, is the disavowal of the word. For this is a racism that denies its proper name, a racism of erasure that place its own name under erasure. Not apartheid, not even ~~apartheid,~~ but rather simply [   ].'
Saree Makdisi, 'Apartheid / Apartheid / [   ]', *Critical Inquiry*, 2018.

4. 'a single settlement peach ...'
'Each settlement peach consumed by British citizens, for example, contains 140 liters of virtual water appropriated from Palestinians.' Visualizing Palestine and EWASH, 'Not Enough Water in the West Bank?', *Jadaliyya* 26 March 2013. Web.

5. 'from tear gas Made in France by SAE Alestex / hurled also at the gilets jaunes / cannisters, CM6 grenades / G1 'random motion' grenades / impossible to pick up and throw back'
These facts are taken from 'How Lebanese Protesters are Targeted by French Military-Grade Tear Gas' by Kareem Chehayeb, *Middle East Eye*, 27 November 2019. Web.

6. Many of the facts from the section 'collude in the Dead Sea's contraction' to 'more than a settler' come from the following sources: Charlotte Silver, 'Israel's Water Miracle That Wasn't', *Al Jazeera*, 30 March 2014. Web. Sue Surkes, 'Sinking Israel-Jordan Relations Leave Dead Sea, A Natural Wonder, Low and Dry', *Times of Israel*, 7 November 2019. Web.

7. 'today there is more blood than water in Gaza'
This line is a variation of the last line of the poem 'Gaza, from the Diaspora' by Jehan Bseiso, 'There's more blood than water today in Gaza.' *Electronic Intifada*, 28 July 2014. Web.

8. 'colonial difference built ...'
'what Walter Mignolo identifies as the foundational 'colonial difference' on which the world of modernity was to institute itself.' Sylvia Wynter quoting Walter Mignolo in her essay 'Unsettling the Coloniality of Being/Power/Truth/Freedom: Towards the Human, After Man, Its Overrepresentation – An Argument', CR: The New Centennial Review, 2003.

9. 'but for our living / not to be only a problem to be solved'
'When we view our living in the european mode, only as a problem to be solved, we rely solely upon our ideas to make us free, for the white fathers told us it was our ideas alone which were precious. But as we become more and more in touch with our own ancient and original non-european view of living as a situation to be experienced and interacted with, we learn to cherish our feelings, and to respect those hidden and deep sources of our power from whence true knowledge and therefore lasting action come.' Audre Lorde, 'Poetry Makes Something Happen', undated manuscript published for the first time in *I Am Your Sister: Collected and Unpublished Writings of Audre Lorde,* 2009.

10. 'on our terror of the gorgeous void / which only liars fear'
'The liar fears the void.' Adrienne Rich, 'Women and Honor: Some Notes on Lying', 1977.

11. 'in the first person plural'
I am borrowing the idea of the first-person plural from American poet Mark Nowak, described by Margaret Ronda in her review 'First-Person Plural: On Mark Nowak's *Social Poetics*', *Los Angeles Review of Books*, 5 July 2020. Web.

12. 'as if our veins ended in us'
A variation of a line from Roque Dalton's poem 'Like You', translated from Spanish by Jack Hirschman.

13. 'at least / summers are hot in your country!'
I am convinced this is a variation of a line from the following book, but I have failed repeatedly to find it. Mourid Barghouti, *I Saw Ramallah*, translated by Ahdaf Soueif, 2004.

14. The phrase 'whose shit you can literally see from space' and some of the surrounding facts come from Lina Mounzer's, 'Waste Away, Notes on Beirut's Broken Sewage System', *The Baffler*, July 7 2019. Web.

15. 'somebody else's nightmares'
This phrase is from the song 'In These Last Days' by Jeanne Lee, Andrew Cyrille and Jimmy Lyons from the 1979 album *Nuba.*

16. 'that bourgeois phenomenon'
'It is a fact: the *nation* is a bourgeois phenomenon.' Aimé Césaire,

Discourse on Colonialism, translated by Joan Pinkham, 1972.
17. 'give not your life to things / throw things to the flood / all one in the
end – water'
'O my floating life
Do not save love
      for things
            Throw *things*
to the flood'
Lorine Niedecker, 'Paean to Place', *Collected Works,* University of
California Press, 2002.

18. 'What else constantly ceases being what it is not?'
'Consequently, it is time to learn to free ourselves from the Eurocentric
mirror where our image is always, necessarily, distorted. It is time, finally,
to cease being what we are not.'
Anibal Quijano, 'Coloniality of Power, Eurocentrism, and Latin America',
International Sociology, 2000.

19. 'from barbarism to Europe'
'the Europeans generated a new temporal perspective of history and
relocated the colonized population, along with their respective histories
and cultures, in the past of a historical trajectory whose culmination was
Europe. Notably however, they were not in the same line of continuity as
the Europeans, but in another, naturally different category. The colonized
peoples were inferior races and in that manner were the past vis-a-vis the
Europeans.' Anibal Quijano, 'Coloniality of Power, Eurocentrism, and
Latin America', *International Sociology,* 2000.

Acknowledgements

Earlier versions or extracts from poems printed here first appeared in *Zarf, Datableed, No Relevance, Berfrois* and *Granta.*

My gratitude to Jazmine Linklater, Nell Osborne, and Hilary White of No Matter for encouraging my writing, and for giving me the idea to name the Amman poems 'Letters from...'.

Thank you to Lotte L.S. for her kind and rigorous feedback on the poem 'Affiliation'.

For bringing these poems into the world so beautifully and for their patience, kindness and editorial vision I thank Jo Lindsay Walton and Samantha Walton.

Thanks also to Ellen, Cai, Sarona, Emilia and my family.